Bank Tellers: Banking Teller Supervisor: Formulas, Principles & References: Last Minute Revision Guide For Success at Any Banking Client Service Specialist Job Interviews and Exams

A Note from the Author:

Why this Book:
The average day for a bank teller requires a wide variety of skills for a variety of responsibilities.
This book tries to bring together the important information for a last minute preparation in as low as 60 minutes. In this book you will get formulas & references for a bank teller job. It has been well written to make it a very quick read. You may find that some of the formulas are presented in different formats that can help you memorize and understand them. This book tries to provide answers to questions asked during interview for various Bank Teller job related information and formulas for Balance , Checking and Savings , Bank Products and Services, Currency Logs, Customer Inquiries , FICA Payments, Bank Policies and Procedures, Money Orders and Cashier's Checks, Loan Payments, Withdrawals etc… etc. It also covers non-technical, HR and Personnel questions in brief.

Good Luck,
Robert J Davis

*****

Buy with Confidence (Read sample before you buy the book...)

Copy Right
Kumar
BLGS LLC
USA

All rights reserved. No part of this may be used or reproduced in any form or by any means, or stored in a database or retrieval system, or transmitted or distributed in any form by any means, electronic, mechanical photocopying, recording or otherwise, without the prior written permission of author or publisher. The information provided is for only instructional value. This book is sold as is, without warranty of any kind, either expresses or implied. This e-book is provided "as is" without warranty of any kind, either express or implied, including, but not limited to, the implied warranties of merchantability, fitness for a particular purpose, or non-infringement. In no event shall the authors or copyright holders, publisher, distributor be liable for any claim, damages or other liability, whether in an action of contract, tort or otherwise, arising from, out of or in connection with the book or the use or other dealings in the book.

This publication could include technical inaccuracies or typographical errors. Changes are periodically added to the information herein; these changes will be incorporated in new editions of the publication. While every precaution has been taken in the preparation of this book, the publisher and the author assume no responsibility for errors or omissions. Neither is any liability assumed for damages resulting from the use of the information or instructions contained herein. It is further stated that the publisher and author are not responsible for any damage or loss to your data or your equipment that results directly or indirectly from your use of this book. All products mentioned in this book are trademarks, registered trademarks or service marks of the companies referenced in this book. This note is not sponsored, endorsed or affiliated by any associated vender.

Trademarks: All trademarks are the property of their respective owners; BLGS LLC is not associated with any product or vendor mentioned in this book.
Disclaimer:
This book is generic books for no particular Bank please check with human resources department to find out their requirements.

INDEX

BANK TELLERS: BANKING TELLER SUPERVISOR: FORMULAS, PRINCIPLES & REFERENCES: LAST MINUTE REVISION GUIDE FOR SUCCESS AT ANY BANKING CLIENT SERVICE SPECIALIST JOB INTERVIEWS AND EXAMS

Bottom Line job interview question

Interview Question that may be asked?

What personal attributes you have to be a bank teller?

As a Bank Teller how will you greet your customers?

What work ethics makes you a good Bank Teller?

What skills you have that can help increase customer satisfaction?

What would you verify for check cashing service?

How can you assess credit risk of a Loan?

How will you know if a customer can repay the loans on time?

Are you familiar with credit reporting agencies? What they do?

What kind of depository institutions you have worked with?

Do you know how banks make money?

Do you know how banks use their funds?

Do you know during a teller's exchange, what does the seller keep?

When will you use Suspicious Activity Report (SAR)?

Do you know what causes returned checks?

- How will you handle Bank Teller's responsibilities as Cashier?
- What strategy is used by banks to increase their profitability?
- How U.S. regulators determine the soundness of Banks and financial institutions?
- What is the relationship between assets and liabilities?
- Which Bank Security operations you are familiar with?
- What Types of Pension Plans you have worked with?
- What factors you will consider while Benefits Calculation?
- What kind of risks you are familiar in banking?
- Explain your experience with MIL; Monetary Instrument Log?
- What kind of endorsement you are aware of?
- Explain your experience with Credit and Debit?
- Explain Overage?
- When will you use Currency Transaction Report – (CTR)?
- Explain your experience with Color Shifting Ink?
- Designing and printing U. S. currency is done by whom?
- What is the Basic Accounting Equation?
- Are you familiar with FICA?
- What you know about the employer matching of FICA?
- What is your experience with Financial Inventory?
- What is Shadow banking?
- What types of shadow banks you are aware of?

What you know about Disability Income Insurance?

What you know about Pension?

What you know about the contribution age limit for Traditional & Roth IRA?

What you know about Annuity?

What you know about the factors that determine the income an annuitant receives?

What you know about the Premium paying methods?

What you know about the various annuity settlement options?

What you know about the six renewal options?

How will you mitigate Banks operational risk?

What you know about the types of financial statements?

Explain your experience with FRS?

What happens when a bank fails?

Explain your experience with 401(k) and 403b?

Where do you store valuables and documents?

How will you calculate Future Value of the 1st payment for an ordinary annuity?

How to calculate Annuity?

How will you calculate Simple Interest?

How will you calculate Relation between Present Value and Future Value?

How will you calculate Future Value of a Single Present Amount?

How will you calculate Future Value of an Ordinary Annuity?

How will you calculate Present Value of a Single Future Amount?

How will you calculate Present Value of an Ordinary Annuity?

How will you calculate Compound Interest?

How will you calculate Effective Interest Rate?

How will you make Taxes and Investment Decisions?

How will you calculate Target Return on Loan?

How will you determine what rate to be used for discounting?

How will you make investment decisions?

What are the responsibilities of Bank Teller as distributor?

What skill you think is most important in dealing with customers?

As a Bank Teller can you share customer's information?

Explain your experience with POD and MICR

How will you stack POD tickets?

What are included in completed POD ticket?

Tell us your experience with using bait money?

What is National Banking Act 1863?

What you know about FHLB?

What factors have shaped the modern banking industry?

What you know about Steagall Act?

What is GLB act?

What is fixed-rate mortgage?

- What is a construction loan?
- What is Lockbox service?
- How will you calculate simple interest?
- How to determine the maturity value of a loan?
- How to calculate Nominal Yield?
- How to calculate Effective interest rate on a discounted interest loan?
- How to calculate Effective interest rate
- How to calculate Loan Price?
- How to calculate Zero Coupon Bonds?
- How to calculate Yield to Maturity?
- How to calculate Effective period interest rate?
- Effective annual yield associated with a periodic interest rate?
- How will you calculate Effective annual yield?
- How will you obtain an effective annual yield associated with a periodic interest?
- How will you calculate loan payment?
- How will you Calculate Total Deposits?
- Explain GLBA's Safeguards Rule?
- What does MITF stand for, what is it?
- What is a Wire Transfer Sheet, what is it for?
- How long are we required to keep these records?
- What information needs to be included for a Wire Transfer Sheet?
- How will you calculate Dividend Payout Ratio?

How will you calculate Net Profit Margin?

How will you calculate Quick Ratio?

How will you calculate Return on Equity?

Mathematical Constants

Algebra Formulas

Ratio & Proportion

Formula to calculate Percentage

Arithmetic

Standard Quadratic Function Equation

Simple & Compound Interests

Formulas to calculate Sum

BANK/FINANCE FORMULAS

Non-Technical/Personal/HR interview: Complimentary

Bottom Line Job interview?

Sample Interview Question?

What are your greatest strengths?

What are your greatest weaknesses?

Had you failed to do any work and regret?

Where do you see yourself five years from now?

How Will You Achieve Your Goals?

Why are you leaving Your Current position?

Why are you looking for a new job?

Why should I hire you?

Aren't you overqualified for this position?

Describe a Typical Work Week?

Are You Willing to Travel?

Describe the pace at which you work?

How Did You Handle Challenges?

How do you handle pressure? Stressful situations?

How Many Hours Do You Work?

Why are you the best person for the job?

What are you looking for in a position?

What do you know about our organization?

What are your short term goals?

What Salary are you looking for?

Tell me more about yourself.

Why did you leave your previous job?

What relevant experience do you have?

If your previous co-workers were here, what would they say about you?

Where else have you applied?

What motivates you to do a good job?

Are you good at working in a team?

Has anything ever irritated you about people you've worked with?

Is there anyone you just could not work with?

Tell me about any issues you've had with a previous boss.

Any questions you want to ask?

Why did you choose this career?

What did you learn from your last job experience?

Why is there a gap in your resume?

How do you keep current and informed about your job and the industries that you have worked in?

Tell me about a time when you had to plan and coordinate a project from start to finish?

What kinds of people do you have difficulties working with?

What do you want to be in 5 years?

What is an Ideal career for you?

What responsibilities you expect?

Dream job?

What Skills you have developed?

What sets you apart?

If the project not gone as planned, what actions will you take?

If unable to meet deadlines, what you can do?

What Interpersonal skills you have?

Improve?

What do you feel has been your greatest work-related accomplishment?

Have you ever had to discipline a problem employee? If so, how did you handle it?

Why do you want this position?

Why are you the best person for this job?

What about Technical writing?

How versatile you are? Can you do other works?

How do you manage time?

How do you handle Conflicts?

What kind of supervisory skills you have?

Any Bad Situation you could not solve?

Anything else you want to tell?

About the author

*****

Bottom Line job interview question

Bottom-line: You will learn to answer any questions in such a way that you match your qualifications to the job requirements.

Interview Question that may be asked?

Example response: Try to customize your answers to fit the requirements of the job you are interviewing for.

What personal attributes you have to be a bank teller?

I have these attributes that can assist me in providing good service to customers:

- A. I have all the required skill, knowledge & qualification
- B. Be understanding of people with disabilities
- C. Competence
- D. Confidence
- E. Confidentiality
- F. Courtesy
- G. Manners
- H. Social Conduct
- I. Polite Behaviour
- J. Trustworthiness
- K. Customers care
- L. I am self confident
- M. I am good at helping people
- N. Motivation

As a Bank Teller how will you greet your customers?

A. I will greet customers politely and courteously as they approach counter

B. Good morning!

C. Good afternoon!

D. How can I help you today?

What work ethics makes you a good Bank Teller?

A. Personal Integrity
B. I follow the chain of command
C. Multi-tasking
D. Protecting Confidential Information
E. Punctuality and Time management
F. Respecting the Law
G. Render the same services to people with visual or physical disabilities
H. Etiquette

What skills you have that can help increase customer satisfaction?

A. Cleanliness
B. Confident
C. Courteous
D. Compassionate
E. Credible
F. Friendly
G. Focused
H. Helpful
I. Honest
J. Knowledgeable
K. Organized
L. Professional
M. Responsive
N. Understanding
O. Warmth

What would you verify for check cashing service?

    A. Verify Account
    B. Verify Funds
    C. Verify Signature
    D. Verify Identification
    E. Verify and get officer approval

How can you assess credit risk of a Loan?

By using Five C's of Credit, also called 5 C's of Banking

    A. Collateral
    B. Capacity
    C. Capital
    D. Character
    E. Credit history

How will you know if a customer can repay the loans on time?

I will use:

1. Credit scores
2. FICO

Are you familiar with credit reporting agencies? What they do?

- A. Equifax
- B. Trans union
- C. Experian

These agencies keep a record of consumer's credit transactions.

What kind of depository institutions you have worked with?

- A. Commercial banks
- B. Savings banks
- C. Credit unions

Do you know how banks make money?

    A. Individual deposits & businesses

    B. Borrowing from other financial institutions

    C. Through the financial markets

Do you know how banks use their funds?

    A. Make loans

    B. Purchase marketable securities

    C. Hold cash

Do you know during a teller's exchange, what does the seller keep?

The seller keeps the debit slip

When will you use Suspicious Activity Report (SAR)?

A. I will use Suspicious Activity Report (SAR), to report a suspicious activity.
B. I will use FinCEN BSA E-Filing System to electronically file the SAR.
C. The SAR is required to be filed within 30 calendar days
D. Its filed with the Financial Crimes Enforcement Network (FinCEN)
E. File reports of cash transactions exceeding $10,000

Do you know what causes returned checks?

A. NSF or ISF - Not Sufficient or Insufficient funds
B. UA or NA - Unauthorized or Not Authorized
C. NCI - Non Cash items
D. UCF, UFH or UF - Uncollected Funds Hold

How will you handle Bank Teller's responsibilities as Cashier?

A. I will Balance cash drawer
B. I will Cash checks
C. I will Prepare deposit slips
D. I will Tender cash
E. I will Verify endorsements

What strategy is used by banks to increase their profitability?

A. Relationship banking
B. Relationship banking is used to increase customer loyalty

How U.S. regulators determine the soundness of Banks and financial institutions?

U.S. regulators use CAMELSs scorecard to determine the soundness of financial institutions
There are six factors that are examined:

    A. C - Capital adequacy

    B. A - Asset quality

    C. M - Management quality

    D. E – Earnings

    E. L – Liquidity

    F. S - Sensitivity to Market Risk

What is the relationship between assets and liabilities?

    A. Assets = Liabilities + Shareholders' Equity
    B. Working Capital = Current Assets - Current Liabilities

Which Bank Security operations you are familiar with?

A. Bait money
B. Bank Protection Act
C. Dye pack
D. Embezzlement
E. Extortion
F. Forgery
G. Kiting
H. Money laundering

What Types of Pension Plans you have worked with?

A. Defined contribution plans
B. Defined benefit plans.

What factors you will consider while Benefits Calculation?

A. Years of service
B. Age at retirement
C. Highest salary attained

What kind of risks you are familiar in banking?

A. Credit risk
B. Foreign exchange risk
C. Interest rate risk
D. Liquidity risk
E. Operational risk
F. Sovereign risk
G. Trading risk

Explain your experience with MIL; Monetary Instrument Log?

A. MIL is used to maintain a record of cash purchases of monetary instruments

B. Value totaling $3,000 to $10,000 for Money orders, cashier's checks, traveler's checks

C. It's used by examiners or audit to verify compliance.

D. Monetary Instrument Log is maintained for 5 years

What kind of endorsement you are aware of?

There are five types of personal endorsements:

    A. Blank endorsement
    B. Special Endorsement
    C. Restrictive endorsement
    D. Qualified Endorsement
    E. Conditional endorsement

Explain your experience with Credit and Debit?

A. Debit decreases the account.

B. Debit includes: withdrawals, personal checks, cash advances

C. Credit increases the account.

D. Credit includes: deposits, cash outs, loan payments, cashiers check

E. Examples :
   i. Assets- Decrease   Credit
   ii. Assets- Increase   Debit
   iii. Revenues- Decrease Debit
   iv. Revenues- Increase   Credit

Explain Overage?

A. Overage = Amount by which a sum of money is greater than a previous estimate
B. Surplus
C. Overage is also over budget
D. Overage funds= Excess funds

When will you use Currency Transaction Report – (CTR)?

A. CTR is a report that U.S. financial institutions are required to file.

B. Its file for each deposit, withdrawal, exchange of currency, or other payment or transfer of more than $10,000.

C. The currency transaction report was initiated by the Bank Secrecy Act in 1970.

These are some of CTR Exemptions:

A. A banks domestic operation

B. A federal, state, or local government agency

C. Any entity with governmental authority within the United States

Explain your experience with Color Shifting Ink?

A. Color-shifting ink adds an extra level of security

B. Ink changes color when viewed at different angles

C. A new color shifting ink was used to print the denomination in the lower right hand corner of the bill on 1996 series of $50s and $100s

D. The original ink color shifted from Green to Black.

E. Upon tilting the bill, Green turns Black.

Designing and printing U. S. currency is done by whom?

The U.S. Department of the Treasury through the Bureau of Printing and Engraving

What is the Basic Accounting Equation?

    A. A=L+Se.

    B. Assets = Liabilities + Shareholders' Equity

Are you familiar with FICA?

    A. Federal Insurance Contributions Act (FICA) tax is a United States federal payroll tax.

    B. It's imposed on both employees and employers to fund Social Security and Medicare.

    C. FICA is a cash management solution.

    D. FICA offers a high level of FDIC insurance, competitive yield and no term requirement.

E. FICA with FDIC insurance on all deposits enables depositors to earn competitive yields versus alternative investments.

What you know about the employer matching of FICA?

A. FICA is the acronym for Federal Insurance Contributions Act.

B. FICA requires employers to withhold Social Security and Medicare taxes from their employees' wages.

C. Employers must remit two times the required withholdings for Social Security and Medicare taxes.

What is your experience with Financial Inventory?

A. Financial Inventory is a careful review of finances.

B. Financial Inventory includes the creation of a personal balance sheet and cash flow statement.

What is Shadow banking?

What types of shadow banks you are aware of?

Shadow banks are non-depository institutions providing substitutive services:
        A. Hedge Funds
        B. Insurance Companies
        C. Mortgage Finance
        D. Money Market Funds
        E. Investment Banks

What you know about Disability Income Insurance?

A. Disability income insurance is a form of health insurance

B. It replaces income when the insured is unable to work as a result of illness, injury, or disease

What you know about Pension?

Pension is a fixed amount of money paid to a retired person by:

A. A government

B. Former employer

What you know about the contribution age limit for Traditional & Roth IRA?

A. Traditional IRA contributions must made prior in which the Member turns 70 1/2

B. Members can contribute to this IRA type at any age as long as there is earned income

What you know about Annuity?

A. An annuity is an account in which equal regular payments are made
B. A stream of equal payments at predetermined intervals
C. A regular periodic payment made to policyholder for a specified period of time
D. Purpose of Annuities is the distribution of Lifetime income.

What you know about the factors that determine the income an annuitant receives?

    A. Amount of money available

    B. Gender

    C. Age

    D. Type of annuity

What you know about the Premium paying methods?

    A. Single premium

    B. Installment premium

What you know about the various annuity settlement options?

    A. Cash refund

B. Installment refund
C. Joint and survivor
D. Joint life
E. Life with period certain
F. Straight life
G. Temporary

What you know about the six renewal options?

A. Cancelable
B. Conditionally renewable
C. Guaranteed renewable
D. Non-cancelable
E. Optionally renewable
F. Term

How will you mitigate Banks operational risk?

A. By Security precautions

B. By Monitoring employee actions

C. By Contingency planning

What you know about the types of financial statements?

A. Income Statement

B. Balance Sheet

C. Statement of Cash Flows

D. Statement of Retained Earnings

Explain your experience with FRS?

A. FRS is the Federal Reserve System.
B. It is also known as the Federal Reserve.
C. Informally it is known as the Fed.
D. It is the central banking system of the United States.

There are six Functions of the FRS:

A. FRS Creates money

B. FRS acts as the banker's bank

C. FRS clear checks

D. FRS regulates member banks

E. FRS Provides uniform currency

F. FRS acts as nation's fiscal agent

What happens when a bank fails?

A. A bank is considered failed when it's unable to meet its obligations to its depositors or creditors.

B. In the U.S., deposits in savings and checking accounts are backed by the FDIC up to 250,000$.

C. FDIC steps in to protect insured depositors.

D. FDIC will sale the bank to a healthy bank.

E. FDIC will also directly pay their depositors.

Explain your experience with 401(k) and 403b?

A. A tax-deferred investment and savings plan that acts as a personal pension fund for employees

B. 401(k) plans allow employees to make pre-tax contributions for retirement savings and which may include employer matching contributions

C. A 401(k) plan is a type of employer-sponsored retirement savings plan that is funded by employee contributions and often matching contributions from the employer.

D. 401(k) plans derive their name from the IRS Tax Code Section 401, paragraph (k).

E. This section of the Code allows for tax-qualified deferred compensation from employees.

F. These deferred wages are not subject to income tax withholding at the time of deferral. This allows the funds to grow tax-free until withdrawn, at which point they are taxed.

G. 401(k) plans are generally self-directed and are portable, meaning employees may transfer them upon changing jobs.

H. 403b plans are tax-deferred retirement plans for employees of public school systems, and tax-exempt, nonprofit organizations such as churches and charitable institutions

Where do you store valuables and documents?

A. A bank vault
B. Strong room

How will you calculate Future Value of the 1st payment for an ordinary annuity?

I. $F1 = PMT (1+r/n) m-1$
II. The future value of the next to last payment is $Fm-1 = PMT (1+r/n)$
III. The future value of the last payment is $Fm = PMT$.
IV. The total future value $F = F1 + F2 + F3 + ... + Fm-1 + Fm$

How to calculate Annuity?

Annuity formulas
  I. Simple interest   INT=PVrt

  II. Simple Interest. INT = PVrt.

  III. INT = interest. PV = present value (amount invested or borrowed) r = interest rate as a decimal t = number of years.

  IV. Simple interest   FV=PV(1+rt)

How will you calculate Simple Interest?

The simple interest INT on an investment (or loan) of PV (present value) dollars at an
  I. INT = PVrt

  II. INT = Interest

  III. PV = Present Value

IV. Annual interest rate of r

V. Period of t years

How will you calculate Relation between Present Value and Future Value?

I. Future Value = Present Value + Interest Amount
II. Interest amount = Principal amount x Interest rate

How will you calculate Future Value of a Single Present Amount?

I. Future value = Present amount x $(1 + r)^n$
II. r = Interest Rate
III. n = Number Of Periods

How will you calculate Future Value of an Ordinary Annuity?

    I. Future value = Annuity Amount x $[(1 + r)^n - 1] / r$
    II. r = interest rate
    III. n = number of periods

How will you calculate Present Value of a Single Future Amount?

    A. Present value = Future Amount x $1 / (1 + r)^n$
    B. r = interest rate
    C. n = number of periods

How will you calculate Present Value of an Ordinary Annuity?

    A. Present value = Annuity Amount x $[1 - 1/(1 + r)^n] / r$
    B. r = interest rate
    C. n = number of periods

How will you calculate Compound Interest?

A. The future value of an investment of PV dollars earning interest at an annual rate of r compounded m times per year for a period of t years is FV = PV (1 + r/m) mt

B. FV = PV (1 + i) n

C. Where i = r/m is the interest per compounding period and n = mt is the number of compounding periods.

D. PV = FV/ (1 + r/m) mt

How will you calculate Effective Interest Rate?

A. The effective interest rate is: $r_{eff} = (1 + r/m)^m - 1$.

B. If money is invested at an annual rate r, compounded m times per year

How will you make Taxes and Investment Decisions?

A. After-tax rate = (1 − tax rate) * Before tax Interest rate

B. 1 + Real Rate = (1 + Nominal Interest Rate) / (1 + Rate of Inflation)

C. Real Rate = Nominal Rate − Inflation Rate

How will you calculate Target Return on Loan?

I will use the formula: [(Target ROE/ (1-tax)) X (Equity/Loan)]

How will you determine what rate to be used for discounting?

    A. If cash flows are real cash flows, I will use real rate for discounting

    B. If cash flows are nominal cash flows, I will use nominal rate for discounting

How will you make investment decisions?

    I Invest so as to maximize the net present value of after-tax cash flows, I will use these factors:
    A. Average rate of return (AVR)
    B. Net present value (NPV)

C. Discount factors
D. Time value of money:

What are the responsibilities of Bank Teller as distributor?

To issue:
    A. Bank drafts

    B. Cash advances

    C. Cashier's checks

D. Money orders

E. Savings bonds

F. Traveler's checks

What skill you think is most important in dealing with customers?

A. Flexibility
B. Adapting to a customer's unique needs

As a Bank Teller can you share customer's information?

We can not share it, customers' information is strictly confidential

Explain your experience with POD and MICR

- A. MICR means Magnetic Ink Character Recognition.
- B. MICR Code is a character-recognition technology used by banks.
- C. MICR allows scanning and reading the information directly
- D. POD is Proof is deposit.
- E. POD is also called MICR tickets.
- F. POD is required for every transaction.

How will you stack POD tickets?

- A. Credit first: Deposit, withdrawal, payment slip
- B. Debit Next: Cash in and out tickets
- C. Debit Check

What are included in completed POD ticket?

- A. Current Date

B. Complete customer name and address
C. Account Number
D. Dollar Amount

Tell us your experience with using bait money?

A. I have used the Bait money to aid the tracing of bank robbers.
B. I have used the bait money system as a form of tracking for locating stolen funds.
C. I have used it to enhance the security of the handling of cash.
D. I record the serial numbers of the bait money notes and sign the log.
E. I keep the Bait Money in the Teller desk along with the regular funds.
F. I keep it in such a way that it's readily identified by the cashier.
G. I ensure not to pay out Bait Money to regular customers.
H. I always verify Bait money as part of the cash counts

What is National Banking Act 1863?

I. The National Banking Acts of 1863 and 1864 established a system of national banks
II. United States federal banking acts created the United States National Banking System.
III. It allowed a development of a national currency backed by bank holdings of U.S. Treasury securities.
IV. It established the Office of the Comptroller of the Currency as part of the United States. Department of the Treasury
V. It authorized the Comptroller to examine and regulate nationally chartered banks.

What you know about FHLB?

A. The Federal Home Loan Bank system is made of twelve Federal Home Loan Banks.

B. Government-sponsored bank involved in housing and community economy development.

C. It was created in 1932 by the Federal Home Loan Bank Act.

D. FHLBs provide cash advances to community banks, thrifts, credit unions, and community development financial institutions.

What factors have shaped the modern banking industry?

I. Federal deposit insurance
II. Branching restrictions

What you know about Steagall Act?

I. The Glass-Steagall Act separated commercial and investment banking.

II. The Glass-Steagall Act made it illegal for a commercial bank to buy or sell securities on behalf of its Customers.

What is GLB act?

A. GLB is Gramm-Leach-Bliley Financial Services Modernization Act of 1999
B. It was enacted to protect non public consumer information
C. GLB advises consumers about policies with regard to use and exchange of info
D. Offers consumers the opportunity to limit the use and exchange of personal info
E. GLB Creates a security program to protect personal info from unauthorized release
F. The CFPB - Consumer Financial Protection Bureau is responsible for enforcing it.
G. Non public personal information is personally identifiable financial information provided by a consumer to a financial institution, resulting from any transaction with the consumer

What is fixed-rate mortgage?

These components are fixed
    I. Payments on the loan

  II. Interest rate;

 III. Terms

What is a construction loan?

The construction loan is packaged with a real estate loan:

   I. Real estate
  II. Equipment
 III. Business expansion

What is Lockbox service ?

  A. Lock box is a Bank collection service that allows accounts receivable payments to be sent directly to the bank
  B. Lockbox service is depositing customer payment in Lockbox

How will you calculate simple interest?

I. Interest = Principle x Rate x Time

II. For ordinary simple interest, divide the number of days by 360 days.

III. For exact simple interest, divide the number of days by 365 days.

How to determine the maturity value of a loan?

I. Maturity Value = Principle + Interest
II. M = P + I
III. Bank Discount B = M x D x T
IV. Proceeds P = M - B

How to calculate Nominal Yield?

$$i_n = \frac{C}{F}$$

I. Where: i_c = Current yield
II. C = Annual coupon int. payment
III. F = Face amount of the bond

How to calculate Effective interest rate on a discounted interest loan?

I. EIR = i/Pr

II. Where: EIR = Effective interest rate

  i. i = Interest

How to calculate Effective interest rate

Effective interest rate on an ORDINARY INTEREST loan:
  Formula:

I. EIR = i/P

II. Where: EIR = Effective int. rate

  i. i = Interest

ii. P = Principal

How to calculate Loan Price?

Corresponds to the total amount a borrower will pay for what he borrowed; the total amount due.

    I. $LP = P + i$

Where:
    II. P = Principal

    III. i = interest

How to calculate Zero Coupon Bonds?

A. Zero bonds are bonds which carry no interest but are issued at a deep discount which provides capital gains when they are redeemed at face value.

B. The face value of the bond is the price at which it will be redeemed and which is written on the bond certificate. The discount provided corresponds to the interest paid to the bond.

C. Formula:

$$r = (F \div P)^{1/n} - 1$$

Where:

I. r = Rate of interest

II. F = Face value of the bond

III. P = current price of the bond

IV. n = no. of payment periods

How to calculate Yield to Maturity?

I. Refers to the average return on a debt security if kept until maturity, taking into account the income provided by interest payments as well as capital gains or losses.

$$\text{YTM} = \frac{i + \dfrac{F - P}{n}}{\dfrac{F + P}{t}}$$

Where:

I. P = Present Value

II. F = Maturity value

III. i = Nominal interest

IV. n = no. of years to maturity

V. t = no. of times int. is paid

How to calculate Effective period interest rate?

I. The effective period interest rate is equal to the nominal annual interest rate divided by the number of periods per year n:

II. Effective Period Rate = Nominal Annual Rate / n

Effective annual yield associated with a periodic interest rate?

I. Effective annual yield = $(1 + \text{periodic interest rate})^m - 1$

II. Where m is the frequency of payments per year

How will you calculate Effective annual yield?

I. $Y = [I + (P - M)/N] / (P + M)/2$

Where:
  I. Y = Effective annual yield (rate)
  II. N = Number of periods of compounding in total
  III. M = Amount paid/received at date of purchase/sale
  IV. P = Face/Maturity value (final lump-sum payment)
  V. I = Amount of income received/paid per compounding period

How will you obtain an effective annual yield associated with a periodic interest?

Effective annual yield = $(1 + \text{periodic interest rate})^m - 1$

How will you calculate loan payment?

Number of Periodic Payments (n) = Payments per year times number of years

How will you Calculate Total Deposits?

For calculating the Total Deposits I will consider various kinds of deposits: Demands Deposits, Term Deposits, and Interest and Non-Interest bearing deposits.

I will calculate Total Deposits by using formula:

    I. $B_n = A(1+i)^n + \{P \div i \cdot [(1+i)^n - 1]\}$

Where:
    I. B = Balance
    II. P = Principal
    III. A = Amount
    IV. n = No. of months
    V. i = interest rate/month

Explain GLBA's Safeguards Rule?

    A. It requires all financial institutions to design, implement and maintain safeguards

    B. Creates policies and procedures to ensure the security and confidentiality of customer information

C. Protect customer information against unauthorized access.

What does MITF stand for, what is it?

A. Monetary Instrument Transaction form

B. It's a record of all transactions between $3,000 and $10,000 other than cash transactions. MO, cashier checks.

What is a Wire Transfer Sheet, what is it for?

How long are we required to keep these records?

A. It keeps track of all wired transactions made within the bank.

B. Required to keep records for 5 years

What information needs to be included for a Wire Transfer Sheet?

A. Name, address, amount of payment order
B. Date order was made, beneficiary's bank, payment instructions to payee

How will you calculate Dividend Payout Ratio?

I will use the formula: Dividends / net income

How will you calculate Net Profit Margin?

I will use the formula: Net income / net sales

How will you calculate Quick Ratio?

I will use the formula: (Liquidity) = (Cash + Short Term Investment + Ar) / Current Liabilities

How will you calculate Return on Equity?

I Will Use the Formula :(Profitability) =Net Income / Stockholders Equity

Mathematical Constants

A. √2   1.41

B. √3   1.73

C. √4   2

D. √5   2.23

E. The Golden Ratio (Phi, φ) 1.6180339887

F. Euler's Constant = 0.57721 56649 01532 86061

G. e =2.71828 18284 59045 23536 02874 71352 66249 77572 47093 69996

H. Pi (π) 3.1415926535...

I. √-1   Imaginary Unit (i)

J. 2.29558...   The parabolic constant (P2)

K. √2   Pythagoras' constant

L. √3   Theodora's' constant

M. 0.62432   Golomb-Dickman constant (λ, μ)

N. 0.35323...   Hafner-Sarnak-McCurley constant (σ)

O. 4.66920...   Feigenbaum constant (δ)

P. 0.66016...   Twin prime constant (C2)

Q. 0.30366...   Gauss-Kuzmin-Wirsing constant (λ)

R. 1.45136...   Ramanujan-Soldner constant (μ)

S. 0.28016...   Bernstein's constant (β)

T. 1°   π/180 radians

U. 1 rad   180°/π

Algebra Formulas

A. $a^2-b^2 =$ $(a-b)(a+b)$

B. $a^3-b^3=(a-b)(a^2+ab+b^2)$

C. $a^3+b^3=$ $(a+b)(a^2-ab+b^2)$

D. $(a+b)^2 = a^2 + 2ab + b^2$

E. $(a-b)^2 = a^2 - 2ab + b^2$

F. $(a+b)^3 = a^3 + 3a^2b + 3ab^2 + b^3$

G. $(a-b)^3 = a^3 - 3a^2b + 3ab^2 - b^3$

H. Difference of Two Squares $\quad u^2 - v^2 = (u+v)(u-v)$

I. Perfect square trinomial $\quad u^2 + 2uv + v^2 = (u+v)^2$

J. $u^2 - 2uv + v^2 = (u-v)^2$

K. Sum or Difference of Two Cubes

$$u^3 + v^3 = (u+v)(u^2 - uv + v^2)$$

$$u^3 - v^3 = (u-v)(u^2 + uv + v^2)$$

Ratio & Proportion

A proportion is an equation stating that two ratios are equal.

I. If $a : b = c : d$ then

II. $ad = bc$

III. $b/a - d/c$ (Invertendo)

IV. $a/c - b/d$ (Alternandci)

V. $d/b - c/a$

VI. $[(a + b)/b] = [(c + d)/d]$ (Componendo)

VII. $[(a - b)/b] = [(c - d)/d]$ (Dividendo)

VIII. $[(a + b)/(a - b)] = [(c + d)/(c - d)]$ (Componendo and Dividendo)

IX. $[(ka + lb)/(ma + nb)] - [(kc + ld)/(mc + nd)]$

Formula to calculate Percentage

A percentage is a number or ratio as a fraction of 100.

Percent Change, as a decimal = (New - Old)/Old

$N = (1 + G) O;$

N = New Value, 0 = Old Value, G = Growth Rate as decimal

I. If X is R% more than Y=>

   Then Y is less than X by R / (100+R) * 100

II. If X is R% less than Y=>

   Then Y is more than X by R / (100-R) * 100

III. If the price of a commodity goes up by R%,

   Then reduction in consumption will be R/ (100+R)*100,

   To not to increase the expenditure.

IV. If the price of a commodity decreases by R%,

   Then the increase in Consumption: R/ (100-R)*100,

   To not to decrease the expenditure.

Arithmetic

A. Average = (Sum of items)/Number of items

B. Sum of first n natural numbers = $n(n+1)/2$

C. Sum of first n natural odd numbers = n^2

D. Sum of the cubes of first n natural numbers = $[n(n+1)/2]^2$

E. Sum of the squares of first n natural numbers = $n(n+1)(2n+1)/6$

I. H.C.F stands for Highest Common Factor

II. The other names for H.C.F are Greatest Common Divisor (G.C.D) and Greatest Common Measure (G.C.M).

III. The H.C.F. of two or more numbers is the greatest number that divides each one of them exactly.

IV. The least number which is exactly divisible by each one of the given numbers is called their L.C.M.

V. Two numbers are said to be co-prime if their H.C.F. is 1.

VI. H.C.F. of fractions = H.C.F. of numerators/L.C.M of denominators

VII. L.C.M. of fractions = G.C.D. of numerators/H.C.F of denominators

VIII. Product of two numbers = Product of their H.C.F. and L.C.M.

IX. Profit & Loss :

   a. Gain = Selling Price(S.P.) - Cost Price(C.P)

   b. Loss = C.P. - S.P.

   c. Gain % = Gain * 100 / C.P.

d. Loss % = Loss * 100 / C.P.

e. S.P. = (100+Gain %) /100*C.P.

f. S.P. = (100-Loss %) /100*C.P.

X. Time & Work:

   a. If X does a piece of work in n days, then X's 1 day's work = 1/n

   b. If X and Y work together for n days, then (X+Y)'s 1 day's work = 1/n

   c. If X is twice as good workman as Y, then ratio of work done By X and Y = 2:1

Standard Quadratic Function Equation

A. y=ax2+bx+c

B. f(x) =ax2+bx+c

C. ax2 Quadratic term

D. bx Linear term

E. c   Constant term

Simple & Compound Interests

I. Simple interest charge is always based on the original principal:

Simple Interest = (P*N*R)/100

II. Compound interest is interest that is paid on both the principal and also on any interest from past years:

Compound Interest = $P(1 + R/100)^N - P$

III. Amount = Principal + Interest

Where:

P = Principal

R = Interest Rate Percent per Annum

N = Time Period

Formulas to calculate Sum

I. The sum of first n natural numbers = $n(n+1)/2$

II. The sum of squares of first n natural numbers = $n(n+1)(2n+1)/6$

III. The sum of first n even numbers = $n(n+1)$

IV. The sum of first n odd numbers = n^2

V. Sum of the first n square numbers = $n(n+1)(2n+1)/6$

BANK/FINANCE FORMULAS

A. Dividend Yield = Dividends per Share / Price of Stock
B. Dividend Yield = Dividend per Share (/) Market Price per Share
C. Dividend Yield = Dividend per Share (/) Market Price per Share
D. EBIT = Revenue - Operating Expenses
E. Earnings Yield = Earnings per Share (/) Market Price per Share
F. Earnings Yield = Earnings per Share (/) Market Price per Share
G. Earnings per Share = Net Income/Average Shares Outstanding
H. Effective interest rate = discount %/(100-discount %) X 360/(FT - DP)

> Where:
> FT = the full term allowed for payment in days
> DP = the discount period allowed for payment in days

I. Enterprise Value = Market Capitalization + Net Debt - (Cash + Cash Equivalents)
J. Enterprise Value per EBITDA = Enterprise Value/EBITDA
K. Enterprise Value per Earnings = Enterprise Value/Earnings
L. Equity Ratio = (Total Equity)/ (Total Assets)
M. Equity Ratio = Total Equity/Assets
N. Equity Ratio = Total Equity/Total Assets
O. Equity--Ending = Equity--Beginning + Net Income - Withdrawal
P. Financial Leverage = Assets / Equity
Q. Financial Leverage Percentage = Return On Equity - Return on Assets
R. Inventory-on-Hand Period = 365 ÷ (Cost of Good Sold / Inventory)
S. Asset Turnover = Net Sales ÷ Total Assets

T. Quick Ratio= (Cash + Marketable Securities + Accounts Receivable) ÷ Current Liabilities
U. Curent Ratio=Current Assets ÷ Current Liabilities
V. Accounts Payable Turnover = Cost of Goods Sold ÷ Accounts Payable
W. Days Payable Period = 365 ÷ Cost of Good Sold/Accounts Payable
X. Interest Coverage Ratio=Net Income before Taxes + Interest Expense ÷ Interest Expense
Y. Firm's Operating Cycle= Days Sales in Receivables (+) Days Sales in Inventory
Z. Fixed Assets Turnover Ratio= Net Sales (/) Average Total Assets
AA. Form 4 = Inside ownership report filed with the SEC that lists insiders who are buying or selling their company stock
BB. Form 8-K = A report filed with the SEC if significant, non-recurring event occurs before a 10-Q is due.
CC. Form 10-K = A report filed with the SEC from publicly traded companies.
DD. Form 10-Q = A quarterly report, required by the SEC from publicly-traded companies
EE. Form 13-D = An inside ownership report filed with the SEC when an investor acquires more than 5 percent of a company's stock
FF. GP%= GP/Total Sales
GG. General Statement of Leverage= Degree of Leverage (=) Pre-Fixed-Cost Income Amount (/) Post-Fixed-Cost Income Amount
HH. Gross Profit Formula= Gross Profit/Sales Revenue
II. Gross Profit= Sales - Cost Of Goods Sold
JJ. Gross Profit= Sales- COGS
KK. Interest =Loan Amount (Principal) X Rate% X Years (Or Fraction Thereof)
LL. Interest formula=Loan amount (or principal) x rate % x years
MM. Inventory Turnover Ratio= Cost of Goods Sold Equation/Average Inventory
NN. Inventory Turnover= Cost of Sales / Average Inventory
OO. Liabilities = Assets - Owner's Equity

PP. Long-Term-Debt-To-Equity Ratio= Long-Term Debt (/) Stockholders' Equity
QQ. Margin = Net Income / Sales
RR. Mark-Up Rate= Selling Price - Cost Price / Cost Price
SS. Mark-Up= Mark-Up Rate (MR) - Cost Price
TT. Market to Book Ratio= Market Price per Share (/) Book Value per Share
UU. Market to Book Ratio= Market Price per Share (/) Book Value per Share
VV. Net Income = ROI x Average Total Assets
WW. Net Income= Gross Profit - Expenses
XX. Net Profit Margin= Net Income/Net Sales
YY. Net Working Capital Ratio=Current Assets (-) Current Liabilities (/) Total Assets
ZZ. Contribution Margin Ratio=Contribution Margin / Sales
AAA. Break Even=occurs when operating profit equals $0.
BBB. Break Even Quantity in Units= Total Fixed Costs / Contribution Margin per Unit
CCC. Break Even in Sales Dollars=Total Fixed Costs / Contribution Margin Ratio (%)
DDD. Margin of Safety=Current Sales (budget sales)- Computed Break-even
EEE. Contribution Margin=sales - variable costs
FFF. Break Even (Units)= Fixed Costs ÷ Contribution Margin
GGG. Break Even (Sales)= Break Even (Units) × Selling Price
HHH. Profit target level (sales)= sales (units) × selling price
III. Profit Amount=(volume (units) × contribution margin) - fixed costs
JJJ. Return on Invested Capital= [EBIT * (1-tax)] / [BV debt + BV equity - cash]
KKK. GDP Deflator (equation)= GDP Deflator = (Nominal GDP/Real GDP) X 100

LLL. Double-Declining Balance Method = Book Value × (2 ÷ Useful Life)

MMM. Mixed Cost Formula can be stated as $Y = a + bX$

"Y" = total mixed cost
"a" = total fixed cost
"b" = variable cost per unit
"X" = Number of units

NNN. Bond Interest Expense Formula — Face Value x Coupon Rate

OOO. Carrying Value of Bond — Face Value +- Discount or Premium of Bond

PPP. Pension - EPBO = APBO + PV of expected future benefits not yet vested

QQQ. Ratio Analysis - AR Turnover — Credit Sales/Avg AR (Beg + Ending)/2

RRR. Ratio Analysis - Current Ratio — Current Assets/Current Liabilities

SSS. Ratio Analysis - Debt/Equity Ratio — Total Liabilities/Total Equity

TTT. Ratio Analysis - Return on Equity — Net Income/Avg Equity for the Period

UUU. A/R Turnover — Net Credit Sales ÷ Average Net A/R

VVV. A/R Turnover In Days — 365 ÷ A/R Turnover

WWW. Cash Ratio — (Cash Equivalents + Marketable Securities) ÷ Current Liabilities

XXX. Current Ratio — Current Assets ÷ Current Liabilities

YYY. Debt Ratio — Total Liabilities ÷ Total Assets

ZZZ. DuPont Return On Assets — Net Profit Margin X Total Asset Turnover

AAAA. Inventory Turnover — COGS ÷ Average Inventory

BBBB. Inventory Turnover In Days 365 ÷ Inventory Turnover
CCCC. Net Profit Margin Net Income ÷ Net Sales
DDDD. Operating Cycle A/R Turnover In Days + Inventory Turnover In Days
EEEE. Return On Total Assets = Net Income ÷ Average Total Assets
FFFF. Total Asset Turnover = Net Sales ÷ Average Total Sales
GGGG. Working Capital= Current Assets - Current Liabilities
HHHH. Working Capital Turnover= Sales ÷ Average Working Capital
IIII. Net Working Capital= Current Assets - Current Liabilities
JJJJ. Net Working Capital= Current Assets - Current Liabilities
KKKK. One Day's Sales Formula=Net Sales On Account/365
LLLL. Operating Income To Sales =EBIT / Net Sales
MMMM. Owner's Equity = Assets - Liabilities
NNNN. Price To Earnings Ratio = Market Price Per Share (/) Earnings Per Share
OOOO. Quick Ratio= Total Quick Assets / Total Current Liabilities
PPPP. Ratio Of Operating Cash Flow To Current Debt Obligations =
QQQQ. Operating Cash Flow / (Current Maturity Of Long-Term Debt + Notes Payable)
RRRR. ROI = Net Income / Average Total Assets
SSSS. Avoidable Interest=Average Accumulated Expenditures X Interest Rate X Period
TTTT. Receivable Turnover Ratio= Net Sales/Average Net Receivables
UUUU. Return On Assets = Net Income/Average Total Assets
VVVV. Return On Assets(R O A) = Net Income (/) Average Total Assets
WWWW. Return On Assets= Net Income / Average Total Assets

XXXX. Return On Assets = ROA = Net Income (/) Average Total Assets

YYYY. Return On Common Equity (ROCE) = Net Income (-) Preferred Dividends

ZZZZ. Return On Equity = ROE = Net Income (/) Average Total Equity

AAAAA. Return On Equity = Net Income (/) Average Total Equity

BBBBB. Return On Investment = Earnings/Enterprise Value

CCCCC. Sales = Average Total Assets X Turnover

DDDDD. Selling Price = Cost Price + (Mark-Up Rate X Cost Price)

EEEEE. The Debt Ratio = Total Liabilities / Total Assets

FFFFF. The Debt To Equity Ratio = Total Liabilities / Shareholders Equity

GGGGG. Times Interest Earned = Earnings Before Interest And Taxes / Interest Expense

HHHHH. Total Assets Turnover Ratio = Net Sales (/) Average Total Assets

Non-Technical/Personal/HR interview: Complimentary

Bottom Line Job interview?

Bottom-line: You will learn to answer any questions in such a way that you match your qualifications to the job requirements.

Sample Interview Question?

Example response: Try to customize your answers to fit the requirements of the job you are interviewing for.

What are your greatest strengths?

   I. Articulate.
   II. Achiever.
   III. Organized.
   IV. Intelligence.
   V. Honesty.
   VI. Team Player.
   VII. Perfectionist.
   VIII. Willingness.
   IX. Enthusiasm.
   X. Motivation.
   XI. Confident.
   XII. Healthy.
   XIII. Likeability.
   XIV. Positive Attitude.

XV. Sense of Humor.
XVI. Good Communication Skills.
XVII. Dedication.
XVIII. Constructive Criticism.
XIX. Honesty.
XX. Very Consistent.
XXI. Determination.
XXII. Ability to Get Things Done.
XXIII. Analytical Abilities.
XXIV. Problem Solving Skills.
XXV. Flexibility.
XXVI. Active in the Professional Societies.
XXVII. Prioritize.
XXVIII. Gain Knowledge by Reading Journals.
XXIX. Attention to details.
XXX. Vendor management skills.
XXXI. Excellent Project Management skills.
XXXII. Self-disciplined.
XXXIII. Self-reliant.
XXXIV. Self-starter.
XXXV. Leadership.
XXXVI. Team-building.
XXXVII. Multitasking.
XXXVIII. Prioritization.
XXXIX. Time management.
XL. Can handle multiple projects and deadlines.
XLI. Thrives under pressure.
XLII. A great motivator.
XLIII. An amazing problem solver.
XLIV. Someone with extraordinary attention to detail.
XLV. Confident.
XLVI. Assertive.
XLVII. Persistent.
XLVIII. Reliable.
XLIX. Understand people.
L. Handle multiple priorities.
LI. Build rapport with strangers.

What are your greatest weaknesses?

I. I am working on My Management skills.
  II. I feel I could do things on my own in a faster way without delegating it.
  III. Currently I am learning to delegate work to staff members.
  IV. I have a sense of urgency and I tend to push people to get work done.
  V. I focus on details and think thru the process start to finish and sometimes miss out the overall picture, so I am improving my skills by laying a schedule to monitor overall progress.

Had you failed to do any work and regret?

  I. I have No Regrets.
  II. I am Moving on.

Where do you see yourself five years from now?

  I. I am looking for a long-term commitment.
  II. I see a great chance to perform and grow with the company.
  III. I will continue to learn and take on additional responsibilities.
  IV. If selected I will continue rise to any challenge, pursue all tasks to completion, and accomplish all goals in a timely manner.
  V. I am sure if I will continue to do my work and achieve results more and more opportunities will open up for me.
  VI. I will try to take the path of progression, and hope to progress upwards.
  VII. In the long run I would like to move on from a technical position to a management position where I am able to smoothly manage, delegate and accomplish goals on time.
  VIII. I want to Mentor and lead junior-to-mid level reporting analysts.

IX. I want to enhance my management experience in motivating and building strong teams.
X. I want to build and manage relationships at all levels in the organization.
XI. I want to get higher degree, new certification.

How Will You Achieve Your Goals?

Advancing skills by taking related classes, professional associations, participating in conferences, attending seminars, continuing my education.

Why are you leaving Your Current position?

I. More money
II. Opportunity
III. Responsibility
IV. Growth
V. Downsizing and upcoming merger, so I made a good, upward career move before my department came under the axe of the new owners.

Why are you looking for a new job?

I have been promoted as far as I can go with my current employer.
I'm looking for a new challenge that will give me the opportunity to use my skills to help me grow with the company.

Why should I hire you?

I. I know this business from ground up.
II. I have Strong background in this Skill.
III. Proven, solid experience and track record.

IV. Highest level of commitment.
V. Continuous education on current technical issues.
VI. Direct experience in leading.
VII. Hands-on experience.
VIII. Excellent Project Management skills.
IX. Demonstrated achievements.
X. Knowledge base.
XI. Communications skills.
XII. Ability to analyze, diagnoses, suggests, and implements process changes.
XIII. Strong customer service orientation.
XIV. Detail oriented, strong analytical, organizational, and problem solving skill.
XV. Ability to interact with all levels.
XVI. Strong interpersonal, relationship management skills.
XVII. Ability to work effectively with all levels, cultures, functions.
XVIII. I am a good team player.
XIX. Extensive Technical experience.
XX. Understanding of Business.
XXI. Result and customer-oriented.
XXII. Strong communication skills.
XXIII. Good Project and Resource management skills.
XXIV. Exceptional interpersonal and customer service skills.
XXV. Strong analytical, evaluative, problem-solving abilities.
XXVI. Good management and planning skills.
XXVII. Good Time Management skills.
XXVIII. Ability to work independently.
XXIX. I've been very carefully looking for the jobs.
XXX. I can bring XX years of experience.
XXXI. That, along with my flexibility and organizational skills, makes me a perfect match for this position.
XXXII. I see some challenges ahead of me here, and that's what I thrive on.
XXXIII. I have all the qualifications that you need, and you have an opportunity that I want. It's a 100% Fit.

Aren' t you overqualified for this position?

I. In My opinion in the current economy and the volatile job market overqualified is a relative term.
II. My experience and qualifications make me do the job right.
III. I am interested in a long term relationship with my employer.
IV. As you can see my skills match perfectly.
V. Please see my longevity with previous employers.
VI. I am the perfect candidate for the position.
VII. What else can I do to convince you that I am the best candidate? There will be positive benefits due to this. Since I have strong experience in this ABC skill I will start to contribute quickly. I have all the training and experience needed to do this job. There's just no substitute for hands on experience.

Describe a Typical Work Week?

I. Meeting every morning to evaluate current issues.
II. Check emails, voice messages.
III. Project team meeting.
IV. Prioritize issues.
V. Design, configure, implement, maintain, and support. Perform architectural design. Review and analysis of business reports.
VI. Conduct weekly staff meetings.
VII. Support of strategic business initiatives.
VIII. Any duties as assigned. Implementation.
IX. Monitor and analyze reports.
Routine maintenance and upgrades.
X. Technical support.
XI. Deploy and maintain.
XII. Provide day-to-day support as required.
Work with customers and clients.
XIII. Documentation.
XIV. Standard operating procedures.
XV. Tactical planning.
XVI. Determine and recommend.
XVII. Plan and coordinate the evaluation.

XVIII. Effective implementation of technology solutions.
XIX. To meet the business objectives.
XX. Participation in budget matters.
XXI. Readings to Keep Abreast Of Current Trends and Developments in the Field.

Are You Willing to Travel?

I. For the right opportunity I am open to travel.
II. I'm open to opportunities so if it involves relocation I would consider it.

Describe the pace at which you work?

I. I work at a consistent and steady pace.
II. I try to complete work in advance of the deadline.
III. I am able to manage multiple projects simultaneously.
IV. I am flexible with my work speed and try to conclude my projects on time.
V. So far I have achieved all my targets
VI. I meet or exceeded my goals.

How Did You Handle Challenges?

I. Whenever the project got out of track I Managed to get the project schedules back on the track.
II. Whenever there was an issue I had researched the issues and found the solutions.
III. We were able to successfully troubleshoot the issues and solve the problems, within a very short period of time.

How do you handle pressure? Stressful situations?

I. In personal life I manage stress by going to a health club.

    II. I remain calm in crisis.
    III. I can work calmly with many supervisors at the same time.
    IV. I use the work stress and pressure in a constructive manner.
    V. I use pressure to stay focused, motivated and productive.
    VI. I like working in a challenging environment.
    VII. By Prioritizing.
    VIII. Use time management
    IX. Use problem-solving
    X. Use decision-making skills to reduce stress.
    XI. Making a "to-do" list.
    XII. Site stress-reducing techniques such as stretching and taking a break.
    XIII. Asked for assistance when overwhelmed.

How Many Hours Do You Work?

I enjoy solving problems and work as much as necessary to get the job done.
The Norm is 40 hour week.

Why are you the best person for the job?

   I. It's a perfect fit as you need someone like me who can produce results that you need, and my background and experience are proof.
   II. As you can see in My resume I've held a lot of similar positions like this one, and hence I am a perfect fit as all those experiences will help me here.
   III. I believe this is a good place to work and it will help me excel.

What are you looking for in a position?

I. I'm looking for an opportunity where I may be able to apply my skills and significantly contribute to the growth of the company while helping create some advancement and more opportunities for myself.
II. It seems this organization will appreciate my contributions and reward my efforts appropriately to keep me motivated.
III. I am looking for job satisfaction and the total compensation package to meet My Worth that will allow me to make enough money to support my lifestyle.

What do you know about our organization?

I. This is an exciting place to work and it fits my career goals.
II. This company has an impressive growth.
III. I think it would be rewarding to be a part of such a company.

What are your short term goals?

I'd like to find a position that is a good fit and where I can contribute and satisfy my professional desires.

What Salary are you looking for?

I. Please provide me the information about the job and the responsibilities involved before we can begin to discuss salary.
II. Please give me an idea of the range you may have budgeted for this position.
III. It seems my skills meet your highest standards so I would expect a salary at the highest end of your budget.
IV. I believe someone with my experience should get between A and B.

V. Currently I am interested in talking more about what the position can offer my career.
VI. I am flexible but, I'd like to learn more about the position and your staffing needs.
VII. I am very interested in finding the right opportunity and will be open to any fair offer you may have.

Tell me more about yourself.

I. I'm an experienced professional with extensive knowledge.
II. Information tools and techniques.
III. My Education.
IV. A prominent career change.
V. Personal and professional values.
VI. Personal data.
VII. Hobbies.
VIII. Interests.
IX. Describe each position.
X. Overall growth.
XI. Career destination.

Why did you leave your previous job?

I. Relocation.
II. Ambition for growth.
III. This new opportunity is a better fit for my skills and/or career ambitions.
IV. To advance my career and get a position that allows me to grow.
V. I was in an unfortunate situation of having been downsized.
VI. I'm looking for a change of direction.
VII. I want to visit different part of the country I'm looking to relocate.
VIII. I am looking to move up with more scope for progression.

What relevant experience do you have?

I have these XYZ related experience.
I have these skills that can apply to internal management positions et al.

If your previous co-workers were here, what would they say about you?

Hard worker, most reliable, creative problem-solver, Flexible, Helping

Where else have you applied?

I am seriously looking and keeping my options open.

What motivates you to do a good job?

Recognition for a job well done makes me motivated.

Are you good at working in a team?

Yes.

Has anything ever irritated you about people you've worked with?

I've always got on just fine with all my co-workers.

Is there anyone you just could not work with?

No.

Tell me about any issues you've had with a previous boss.

I never had any issues with my boss.

Any questions you want to ask?

Please explain the benefits and bonus.
How soon could I start, if I were offered the job?

Why did you choose this career?

  I. Life style.
  II. Passion.
  III. Desire.
  IV. Interesting.
  V. Challenging.
  VI. Pays Well.
  VII. Demand.

What did you learn from your last job experience?

I gained experience that's directly related to this job.

Why is there a gap in your resume?

Because of Personal and family reasons I was unable to work for some time.
  I. Unemployed.
  II. Job hunt.
  III. Layoffs.

How do you keep current and informed about your job and the industries that you have worked in?

   I.   I pride myself on my ability to stay on top of what is happening in the industry.
   II. I do a lot of reading.
   III. I belong to a couple of professional organizations.
   IV. I have a strong network with colleagues.
   V.   I take classes and seminars.
   VI. I have started and participated in many technical blogs.

Tell me about a time when you had to plan and coordinate a project from start to finish?

   I.   I headed up a project which involved customer service personnel and technicians.
   II.   I organized a meeting and got everyone together.
   III. I drew up a plan, using all best of the ideas.
   IV.   I organized teams.
   V.   We had a deadline to meet, so I did periodic checks with various teams involved.
   VI.   After four weeks, we were exceeding expectations.
   VII. We were able to begin implementation of the plan.
   VIII. It was a great team effort, and a big success.
   IX.   I was commended by management for my managing capacity.

What kinds of people do you have difficulties working with?

   I.   I have worked in very diverse teams.
   II. Diversity means differences and similarities with men and women from very diverse backgrounds and culture. It helps us grow as a human being.
   III. The only difficulty was related to work related dishonesty by a person.

    IV. He was taking credit for all the work our team accomplished.

What do you want to be in 5 years?

I hope to develop my management skills by managing a small staff.

What is an Ideal career for you?

   I. I would like to stay in a field of ABC.
   II. I have been good at ABC.
   III. I look forward to ABC.

What responsibilities you expect?

I would expect expanded responsibilities that could make use of my other skills.

Dream job?

Includes all of the responsibilities and duties you are trying to fill.
I also thrive in the fast changing environment where there is business growth.

What Skills you have developed?

I was very pleased to develop the A, B, C skills that you are seeking.

What sets you apart?

I. Once I am committed to a job or project I take it with tremendous intensity.
II. I want to learn everything I can.
III. I am very competitive and like to excel at everything I do.

If the project not gone as planned, what actions will you take?

Backup and identify precautions.

If unable to meet deadlines, what you can do?

I. Negotiate.
II. Discussion.
III. Restructure.
IV. Redefine Optimum goal.
V. Show a price structure.

What Interpersonal skills you have?

I. I had to learn to say no.
II. Helpful to other staff.
III. Help in return.

Improve?

In any job I hold I can usually find inefficiencies in a process, come up with a solution.

What do you feel has been your greatest work-related accomplishment?

I. Implemented an idea to reduce expenses, raised revenues.
  II. Solved real problems.
  III. Enhanced department's reputation.

Have you ever had to discipline a problem employee? If so, how did you handle it?

  I. Problem-solving skills,
  II. Listening skills, and
  III. Coaching skills.

Why do you want this position?

  I. I always wanted the opportunity to work with a company that leads the industry in innovative products.
  II. My qualifications and goals complement the company's mission, vision and values.
  III. I will be able to apply and expand on the knowledge and experience, and will be able to increase my contributions and value to the company through new responsibilities.

Why are you the best person for this job?

  I. I have extensive experience in XYZ (Skill they are looking for)
  II. I'm a fast learner.
  III. I adapt quickly to change.
  IV. I will hit the ground running.
  V. I'm dedicated and enthusiastic.
  VI. I'm an outstanding performer.

VII. I may be lacking in this specific experience but I'm a fast learner and I'll work harder.

What about Technical writing?

I. I can convert any complex technical information into simple, easy form.
II. I can write reports to achieve maximum results.

How versatile you are? Can you do other works?

I am flexible and can adapt to any changing situations.

How do you manage time?

I. I am very process oriented and I use a systematic approach to achieve more in very less time.
II. I effectively eliminate much paperwork.

How do you handle Conflicts?

I. I am very tactful;
II. I avoid arguments and frictions and
III. I establish trust and mutual understanding.

What kind of supervisory skills you have?

I. I make sure that everyone understands their responsibilities.
II. I try to be realistic in setting the expectations and try to balance the work among all.

Any Bad Situation you could not solve?

I've never yet come across any situation that couldn't be resolved by a determined, constructive effort.

Anything else you want to tell?

    I. I am excited and enthusiastic about this opportunity
    II. I am looking forward to working with you.

About the author/editor/compiler:
Robert J Davis has been involved in the education space for the past 10 years.

Reference:
References were made from accounting journals and manuals.
This is an independent and unauthorized note. No endorsement, sponsorship, affiliation with any other company. Sample questions were analyzed to prepare these notes.
Terms of use and end user agreement:

Access Outside United States :
We make no representation that the materials provided are appropriate or available for use in locations outside of the United States, their territories and possessions. If you use the Services from other locations, you are responsible for compliance with applicable local laws. If you do not agree with this disclaimer, then do not use this. Do not copy. Not one of the document's configurations or suggestions is guaranteed to be suitable for a particular purpose.
Restrictions on use of content per Internet Privacy act.

All rights reserved. You cannot reproduce by any methods such as linking, framing, loading positing to blogs et al, transfer, distribute, rent, share or storage of part or all of the content in any form without the prior written consent of BLGS .its solely for your own non-commercial use. You may not change or delete any proprietary notices from materials received. We assume no responsibility for the way you use the content provided. All these notes files on this site are here for backups for personal use only. If you are sharing any information from here with any third-party you are violating this agreement and Internet Privacy act.
General Jurisdictional Issues:

These Terms of Use will be governed by the laws of the Bucks County in the state of Pennsylvania in USA.
You are responsible for compliance with applicable local laws.
Internet Links This page; Listing or Site may provide links to other Internet sites. You acknowledge that BLGS shall not be responsible or liable, directly or indirectly, for any damage or loss caused or alleged to be caused by or in connection with use of or reliance upon any information, material, products, or services offered or provided through such third-party sites.

Disclaimer of Warranty, No Liability:

LEGAL DISCLAIMERS.
These notes are for job interview. You are encouraged to take proper trainings from the related vendors or buy their books and products.
We do not sell software.
If you need any related software you MUST purchase a legal license copy from software vendor.

DMCA:
All materials here are created with the good faith. All the references if any to copyrighted or trademarked materials are only for references and discussions. These notes do not replace any related vendors documentations. Readers are encouraged to buy and refer to the related vendors documentations and books. These notes are intended for personal use only. The use of any acronym or term on or within any BLGS product, content, website or other documentation should not be considered as impinging on the validity, ownership, or as a challenge to any trademark, logo or service mark. All other trademarks are the property of their respective owners, and the aforementioned entities neither endorse nor sponsor BLGS or its products. All trademarks are

trademarks of their respective owners. All these interview notes Content are not sponsored by, endorsed by or affiliated with any other company. Any Copyright, Confidential Information, Intellectual Property, NDA, or Trademark or Service mark infringements discovered on or within notes and the products and services will be immediately removed upon notification and verification of such activities. Please send your feedback to: bottomline@interview-guru.info

THIS WEB SITE AND THE INFORMATION, CONTENTS, GRAPHICS, DOCUMENTS AND OTHER ELEMENTS INCLUDED HEREIN (COLLECTIVELY THE "CONTENTS") ARE PROVIDED ON AN "AS IS" BASIS WITH ALL FAULTS AND WITHOUT ANY WARRANTY OF ANY KIND. "BLGS" HEREBY DISCLAIMS ALL WARRANTIES AND CONDITIONS WITH REGARD TO THE WEB SITE CONTENTS, INCLUDING WITHOUT LIMITATION, ALL IMPLIED WARRANTIES AND CONDITIONS OF MERCHANTABILITY, FITNESS FOR A PARTICULAR PURPOSE, TITLE AND NON-INFRINGEMENT.

www.ingramcontent.com/pod-product-compliance
Lightning Source LLC
Chambersburg PA
CBHW071821200526
45169CB00018B/548